Winter Fun

Winter Fun

Bible-Based Christmas Activities for Kids

BARBOUR BOOKS

An Imprint of Barbour Publishing, Inc.

Puzzles were prepared by Rebecca Currington, Diane Whisner, and Belinda Mooney in association with Snapdragon Group, Tulsa, Oklahoma, USA.

ISBN 978-1-62836-893-2

Published by Barbour Books, an imprint of Barbour Publishing, Inc., P.O. Box 719, Uhrichsville, Ohio 44683, www.barbourbooks.com

Our mission is to publish and distribute inspirational products offering exceptional value and biblical encouragement to the masses.

Member of the
Evangelical Christian
Publishers Association

Printed in the United States of America.
04720 0814 VP

HEY KIDS

Do you ever look back over the summer and think, "Aargh! The fun ends here!" But not so fast. While the hot, sticky days of summer are over, the joys of winter are just beginning. And think about this: winter lasts twice as long as summer and that means twice as much fun!

This activity book has been created to remind you of all that's fun about winter. From amazing outdoor sports like hockey, sledding, skating, and snowboarding to reading or watching a movie while sipping a cup of hot chocolate, winter has a lot of great things to offer. And you know what else, winter is filled with holidays: Thanksgiving, Christmas, Hanukkah, New Year's Day, Groundhog Day, and President's Day to name just a few. It seems like there's a reason to celebrate waiting around every corner.

In this *Winter Fun* activity book, you will find coloring pages and mazes to enjoy, along with word puzzles, crosswords, puzzles that center around holiday music and stories, dot-to-dots, and picture puzzles. You will also find plenty of activities where you will be asked to take off your mittens and search for answers in the pages of the Bible. When you're through, you will know more than ever before about the birth of our Lord Jesus, the One who is the center of our winter holiday season.

Summer will be back soon enough. Until then, we hope this book will help you eagerly look forward to the thrilling months ahead. Now let's hear a big WAHOO! for winter and all the fun that lies ahead!

Taste of the Holidays

```
C O O K I E S A
G H C N U P W Z
N B E R R I E S
I N A R C H E W
D R P O T A T O
D P L N B M A K
U I U C A K E I
P E M T I U R F
```

cookies	berries	ham
plum	sweet	pie
pudding	potato	fruit
cran	cake	

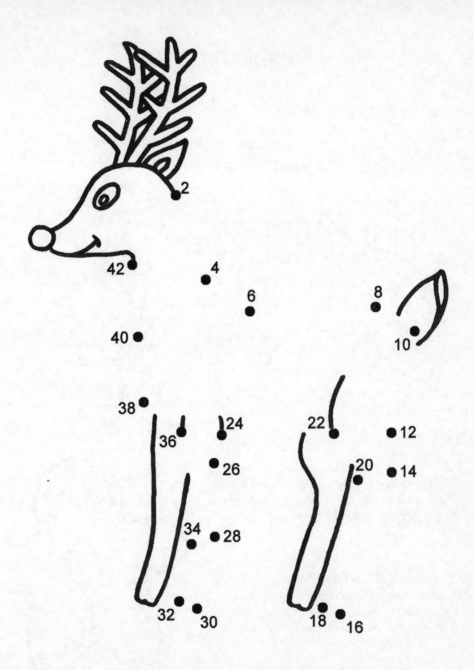

2

42

4

6

8

40

10

38

36   24

22   12

26

20   14

34   28

32   30

18   16

9

COOKIE TIME

1
2
3
G I N G E R B R E A D M A N
4
5
6
7

ACROSS

1. Christmas is a great time to bake ____________.
4. This cookie is made with cinnamon and nutmeg.
6. This cookie sounds like a sandwich with jam.
7. This is a cereal cookie with nuts and raisins.

DOWN

1. This is what you use to shape the cookie dough.
2. You might sprinkle some of these on your cookie dough.
3. This cookie is made from a dark, sticky syrup.
5. This cookie is extra sweet and cut into shapes.

WINTER WARMUPS

Fill in the missing letters to form a word or phrase from top to bottom.

HOT C◯OCOLATE

W◯SSAIL

CA◯S

FIRE◯LACE

FAMIL◯

◯EATERS

GL◯VES

B◯ANKET

M◯TTENS

WOO◯

CO◯TS

JO◯

◯WEATERS

PICTURE THIS

Draw a line from each picture to its matching word in the middle.
When you are through, a few words will be left over. Fill them in
on the lines below to form a phrase

wreath

present

snowman

Christmas tree

Frosty

the

dove

_____ _____ _____

HOLIDAY SONGS

Find the missing words from the list below.

SILENT _____

DO YOU _____ WHAT I HEAR?

JINGLE BELL _____

I'M _____ OF A WHITE CHRISTMAS

WE _____ KINGS

HEAR DREAMING ROCK

NIGHT THREE

WHAT DO YOU KNOW?

A Girl Named Mary

Mary was not just any young woman. God chose her to be the mother of the Christ Child. When God spoke to her, she was willing to do whatever He asked of her. Can you answer these questions?

Whom did God send to Galilee to speak to Mary about the baby she would be having? The answer is hidden in Luke 1:26.

_____

Whom was Mary engaged to when the angel spoke to her? The answer is hidden in Luke 1:27.

_____

Who was the father of Joseph, the husband of Mary, who was Jesus' mother? The answer is hidden in Matthew 1:16.

_____

The angel also told Mary to name her son Jesus, but He would also be called what? The answer is hidden in Luke 1:35.

_____

Winter Weather

```
N  O  S  C  H  O  O  L
S  E  L  C  I  C  I  G
W  F  E  S  N  O  W  L
I  C  E  S  T  A  H  O
N  O  T  M  Q  T  Y  V
D  L  S  Y  A  S  L  E
R  D  P  B  O  O  T  S
W  S  N  E  T  T  I  M
```

snow	icicles	gloves
ice	cold	coats
sleet	boots	mittens
no school	hats	wind

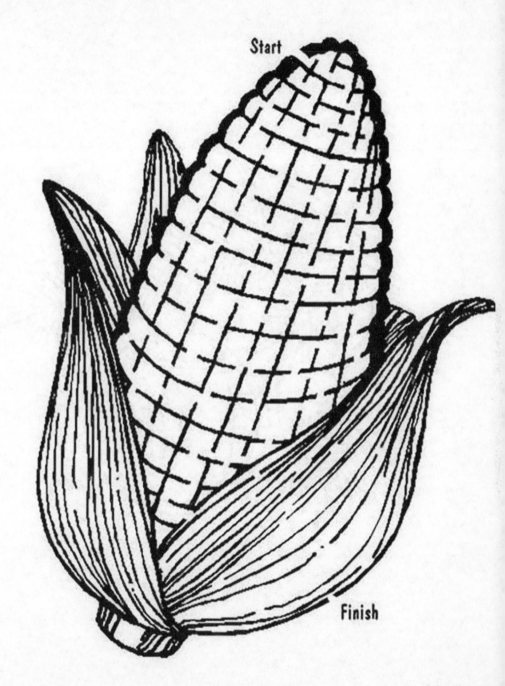

Start

Finish

17

FEBRUARY FORECASTER

Fill in the missing letters to form a word or phrase from top to bottom.

UNDER◯ROUND

BUR◯OW

R◯DENT

CLO◯DY

SU◯NY

PRE◯ICTION

WEAT◯ER

SHAD◯W

EARLY SPRIN◯

WOO◯CHUCK

HOLID◯Y

M◯TH

PICTURE THIS

Draw a line from each picture to its matching word in the
middle. When you are through, a few words will be left over.
Fill them in on the lines below to form a phrase.

snow

of   reindeer

candy cane

dream

angel

stockings

_____ ____ _____

HOLIDAY SONGS

Find the missing words from the list below.

WINTER _____

GOOD _____ WENCELAS

AWAY IN A _____

HAPPY _____ TO YOU

WHILE _____ WATCHED THEIR FLOCKS

MANGER HOLIDAYS KING

SHEPHERDS WONDERLAND

WHAT DO YOU KNOW?

Jesus Is Born

When Jesus was born, Mary and Joseph were not at their home or even in their own city. Can you answer these questions about their journey to Bethlehem?

What powerful ruler said that everyone had to be registered in the cities where they were born? The answer is hidden in Luke 2:1.

_____

Mary and Joseph went to Bethlehem because Joseph was a descendant of what great king?
The answer is hidden in
Luke 2:4.

_____

Mary had her baby while they were on their trip. Why did she wrap up her new baby and lay Him in a manger filled with hay?
The answer is hidden in Luke 2:7.

_____

Winter Games

```
S  N  O  W  M  A  N  S
S  K  A  T  I  N  G  D
W  L  R  Y  L  E  L  F
D  E  L  S  D  M  P  I
K  G  D  F  G  G  Q  G
M  N  Y  E  K  C  O  H
N  A  G  G  O  B  O  T
L  L  A  B  W  O  N  S
```

snowman   angel   snowball
skating   sled   fights
hockey   toboggan

25

THANKSGIVING DINNER

T U R K E Y D A Y F U N

ACROSS
1. These come all mashed up.
6. These come with marshmallows on top.
8. These are saucy in a casserole dish.
9. Apple, cherry, and pumpkin.

DOWN
2. This holiday is a day to give _____ .
3. Pour this over your turkey and dressing.
4. Thanksgiving dinner has all the
   _____.
5. This is stuffed inside the turkey.
7. These are usually chopped up in a sauce.

NIP IN THE AIR

Fill in the missing letters to form a word or phrase from top to bottom.

LONG __OHNS

E__RMUFFS

HOT __HOCOLATE

JAC__ET

MU__FLER

BLUSTE__Y

C__LD SNAP

BRI__K

MIT__ENS

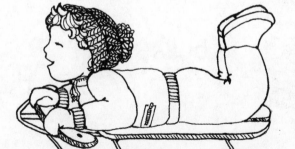

PICTURE THIS

Draw a line from each picture to its matching word in the
middle. When you are through, a few words will be left over.
Fill them in on the lines below to form a phrase.

mistletoe

under

Christmas tree

baby Jesus

candle

bells

the

_____ ____ _____

THANKSGIVING SONGS

Find the missing words from the list below.

NOW THANK WE ALL OUR _____ -

COME, YE THANKFUL _____ COME

WE GATHER _____

WITH _____ HEARTS, O LORD WE COME

COUNT YOUR _____

PEOPLE BLESSINGS GOD

TOGETHER THANKFUL

WHAT DO YOU KNOW?

The Shepherds' Joy

On the night Jesus, the Christ Child, was born, some shepherds were up in the hills taking care of their sheep. All of a sudden, the sky lit up. Can you answer these questions?

Who appeared in the sky and told them not to be afraid?
The answer is hidden in Luke 2:9.

_____

The angel told the shepherds that a baby had been born.
What did the angel call the baby? The answer is hidden in Luke 2:11.

_____

The angels told the shepherds where they could find the baby Jesus.
Where did they say He would be lying?
The answer is hidden in Luke 2:12.

_____

Winter Treats

```
H  L  I  A  S  S  A  W
T  O  W  K  N  M  O  C
G  B  T  C  A  N  D  Y
I  B  I  C  A  N  E  S
N  R  P  L  O  T  P  C
G  E  I  B  S  C  N  B
E  A  E  G  G  N  O  G
R  D  S  K  L  S  S  A
```

ginger	canes	eggnog
bread	pies	wassail
candy	hot cocoa	

WINTER FUN

ACROSS

5. In the winter, the air is ___________.
7. When snow comes in light swirls, the weatherman calls it __________.
8. When the wind blows hard, we say it's ______________.

DOWN

1. White, fluffy stuff that falls from the sky.
2. These are called stones but they are really balls of frozen rain.
3. This makes pretty patterns on the windows.
4. These sparkly things hang from the tree branches and rooftops.
6. When it's really cold outside, we say it's __________.

FUN FUN FUN

Fill in the missing letters to form a word or phrase from top to bottom.

N O R T H __ I N D

I C __

F __ U R R I E S

__ O L D

G L __ V E S

__ I T T E N S

S L __ I G H R I D E S

__ O O L E N S

S K __ I N G

S __ O W B A L L S

C H R I S __ M A S

B __ A U T Y

F __ O S T

PICTURE THIS

Draw a line from each picture to its matching word in the middle. When you are through, a few words will be left over. Fill them in on the lines below to form a phrase.

mittens

turkey

Christmas tree

day

fun   sledding

harvest

_____   _____   _____

WHAT DO YOU KNOW?

The Shepherds Find the Baby

When the angels finished their singing, the shepherds were filled with joy. Can you answer these questions?

What did the shepherds do when the angels disappeared? The answer is hidden in Luke 2:15.

_____

What did the shepherds do on their way home?
The answer is hidden in Luke 2:20.

_____

All About Ice

```
S  O  S  E  T  A  K  S
C  A  P  M  A  E  R  C
R  E  N  Y  W  S  T  R
A  L  B  E  R  G  T  Y
P  C  E  K  L  O  M  S
E  I  I  C  Y  X  Y  T
R  C  F  O  B  A  N  A
F  I  S  H  I  N  G  L
```

berg	fishing	skates
cap	hockey	icicle
crystal	scraper	cream

SALUTE TO WINTER

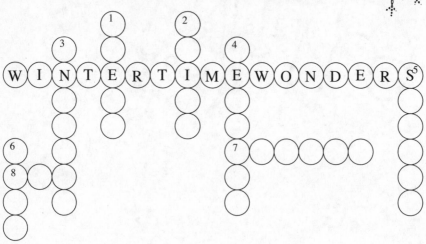

W I N T E R T I M E W O N D E R S

ACROSS

7. A game played with sticks on the ice.
8. When the rain freezes, it becomes _____.

DOWN

1. We ride these down the hills.
2. These are pieces of wood we attach to our feet.
3. These are made by rolling the snow into big balls.
4. Snow, storms, cold, and wind are all kinds of _____.
5. We can glide over the ice with these on our feet.
6. We can't see this, but we feel it when it blows.

THE GREAT OUTDOORS

Fill in the missing letters to form a word or phrase from top to bottom.

SNO __ SHOE

SK __ ING

S __ OWMAN

SKA __ ING

IC __ FISHING

C __ OSS COUNTRY

__ LEDDING

SKI JUM __

H __ CKEY

SNOWBOA __ D

HUN __ ING

BOB __ LED

PICTURE THIS

Draw a line from each picture to its matching word in the middle. When you are through, a few words will be left over. Fill them in on the lines below to form a phrase.

stocking

present

light

the

tree

nutcracker

Christmas

gingerbread man

_____ __ _____ _____

HOLIDAY SONGS

Find the missing words from the list below.

_____ DAYS OF CHRISTMAS

SILVER _____

ROCKIN' AROUND THE CHRISTMAS _____

WHITE _____

THERE'S NO PLACE LIKE _____ FOR THE HOLIDAYS

TREE   CHRISTMAS   HOME

TWELVE   BELLS

WHAT DO YOU KNOW?

Naming the Baby

Mary and Joseph did everything they could for their new baby.
Can you answer these questions?

When Jesus was eight days old, what did His parents name Him?
The answer is hidden in Luke 2:21.

_____

Where did Mary and Joseph take their new son a few days later?
The answer is hidden in Luke 2:22.

_____

What else did Mary and Joseph do while they were in Jerusalem?
The answer is hidden in Luke 2:24.

_____

Winter Wraps

```
O  M  I  T  T  E  N  S
V  N  T  O  C  A  M  W
E  B  L  G  H  R  U  E
R  O  C  A  P  I  F  A
C  O  S  C  A  R  F  T
O  T  M  I  R  O  S  E
A  S  O  C  K  S  N  R
T  E  K  N  A  L  B  F
```

overcoat	scarfmittens	blanket
boots	sweater	muffs
parka	socks	

WINTER WARM-UPS

$$F \quad L^{2} \quad A \quad N \quad N \quad E \quad L \quad N \quad I \quad G^{3} \quad H \quad T \quad G \quad O \quad W \quad N \quad S$$

ACROSS
4. A covering used on a bed.
5. We wear them on our feet when we walk in the snow.
6. These are knit coverings for our hands in cold weather.
7. When we go out to play, we put on our _____.
8. These go around our necks to keep us warm.

DOWN
1. We wear these over our shirts for indoors or outdoors.
2. Men wore these in the old days under their clothes.
3. These are made of cloth or leather and keep our hands warm.

GIVING THANKS

Fill in the missing letters to form a word or phrase from top to bottom.

```
        __EAST
   IND__ANS
       C__ANBERRIES
       __WEET POTATOES
  SWEE__ CORN
       __URKEY
PLYMOUT__
        M__YFLOWER
   BEA__S
   PUMP__IN PIE
       __TUFFING
    VE__ETABLES
   FAM__LY
   HAR__EST
  SHAR__NG
 ACOR__
    PIL__RIMS
```

PICTURE THIS

Draw a line from each picture to its matching word in the middle. When you are through, a few words will be left over. Fill them in on the lines below to form a phrase.

sleigh

present

bells

stocking

ornaments

toys

ring

_____ _____ _____

HOLIDAY SONGS

Find the missing words from the list below.

WE _____ YOU A MERRY CHRISTMAS

UP ON THE _____

THERE'S A _____ IN THE AIR

THE HOLLY AND THE _____

_____ ROASTING ON AN OPEN FIRE

SONG   WISH   IVY

CHESTNUTS   HOUSETOP

WHAT DO YOU KNOW?

Going to the Temple

Mary and Joseph made sure to dedicate Jesus to the Lord. Can you answer these questions?

Whom did Mary and Joseph meet in the Temple in Jerusalem?
The answer is hidden in Luke 2:25.

_____

What did Simeon do when he saw the baby Jesus?
The answer is hidden in Luke 2:28.

_____

Simeon told Mary and Joseph that Jesus would be great and save us all. What did they do when they heard these words?
The answer is hidden in Luke 2:33.

_____

Everyone Loves Snow

```
B S H O V E L M
O H S A W O L P
A O K W E P A S
R E D N U O B T
D N M L F J N O
F L A K E A U R
P A N G E L L M
W H I T E N R L
```

ball   flake   shovel
board   man   storm
bound   plow   angel
fall   shoe   white

THE HOLY BIRTH

ACROSS

7. This is where Mary placed the newborn king.
8. This is the name of Jesus' mother.
9. This is the name of Jesus' earthly father.

DOWN

1. The wise men followed a _____.
2. Mary rode to Bethlehem on a _____.
3. There were no rooms so the baby was born in a _____.
4. Mary and Joseph named the baby _____.
5. There were _____ in the stable.
6. The shepherds and wise men were looking for the _____.

RING IN THE NEW

Fill in the missing letters to form a word or phrase from top to bottom.

HOR __ S

CH __ ERS

T __ ELVE

JANUAR __

GAM __ S

P __ RTIES

FI __ EWORKS

FIR __ T DAY

MI __ NIGHT

H __ TS

HAPP __

PICTURE THIS

Draw a line from each picture to its matching word in the middle. When you are through, a few words will be left over. Fill them in on the lines below to form a phrase.

holiday bells

Christmas tree

noel

first

the

snowflakes

teddy bear

_____ _____ _____

HOLIDAY SONGS

Find the missing words from the list below.

O COME, O COME _____

ALL I WANT FOR CHRISTMAS IS MY TWO _____

THE CHIPMUNK _____

GRANDMA GOT RUN OVER BY A _____

COME ON _____ THOSE BELLS

REINDEER   FRONT TEETH   SONG

EMMANUEL   RING

WHAT DO YOU KNOW?

Also in the Temple

After Simeon blessed Jesus and told His parents about Him, they met a woman named Anna. Can you answer these questions?

How old was the woman Joseph and Mary met in the Temple?
The answer is hidden in Luke 2:37.

_____

What did this woman do all day? The answer is hidden in Luke 2:37.

_____

What did Anna do when she saw Jesus?
The answer is hidden in Luke 2:38.

_____

Winter Words

```
B  F  R  O  S  T  Y  L
Y  L  L  I  H  C  T  X
S  L  U  S  H  M  P  I
P  A  N  S  D  L  O  C
Z  O  T  Y  T  D  L  Y
F  R  E  E  Z  E  A  F
D  N  Y  T  F  A  R  D
F  R  I  G  I  D  S  Y
```

blustery	drafty	frigid
chilly	freeze	frosty
cold snap	polar	icy
	slush	

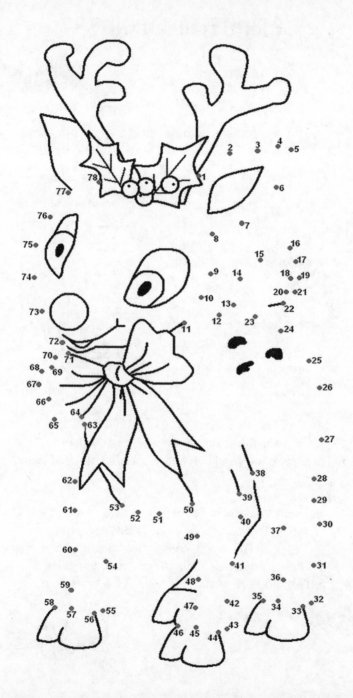

65

CHRISTMAS CANDY

C H O C O L A T E C A R A M E L S

ACROSS

5. These tangy candies look like little white pillows.
6. This is thick, sugary candy cut into squares.
7. These are chewy and come in shapes like fish and bears.

DOWN

1. You break this candy into pieces. It usually has peanuts.
2. These chewy candies come in different colors.
3. This candy comes on a stick.
4. These Christmas candies have stripes and hooks.
5. This old-fashioned candy sounds like it has fruit.

THE HIGHEST OFFICE

Fill in the missing letters to form a word or phrase from top to bottom.

__ A T R I O T S

F E B __ U A R Y

R __ A G A N

W A __ H I N G T O N

L __ N C O L N

L E A __ E R S

J E F F __ R S O N

C L I __ T O N

B I R __ H D A Y S

B U __ H

H O L I __ A Y

O B __ M A

K E N N E D __

PICTURE THIS

Draw a line from each picture to its matching word in the middle. When you are through, a few words will be left over. Fill them in on the lines below to form a phrase.

God

snowman

Christmas tree

gingerbread house

bells

to

thanks

_____ _____ _____

HOLIDAY SONGS

Find the missing words from the list below.

IT'S THE MOST _____ TIME OF THE YEAR

WHAT _____ IS THIS?

GO TELL IT ON THE _____

DECK THE _____

JOY TO THE _____

CHILD   HALLS   WORLD

MOUNTAIN   WONDERFUL

Merry Christmas

WHAT DO YOU KNOW?

Who Is Jesus?

Jesus, the Christ Child, is the most important person in all the Bible. Long before He was born, God told people about Him. Can you answer these questions?

What name did God give to Jesus?
The answer is hidden in Isaiah 7:14.

_____

What does the Bible say will be upon Jesus' shoulders?
The answer is hidden in Isaiah 9:6.

_____

What tribe or clan does the Bible say Jesus will come from?
The answer is hidden in Micah 5:2.

_____

Staying Warm

```
B H E A T D F H
L S T K I O L O
A E H E C O A T
N C R C F W N C
K E O H N E N O
E E W D G R E C
T L I U Q I L O
M F E R I F N A
```

blanket	fleece	throw
quilt	firewood	coat
flannel	heat	hot cocoa

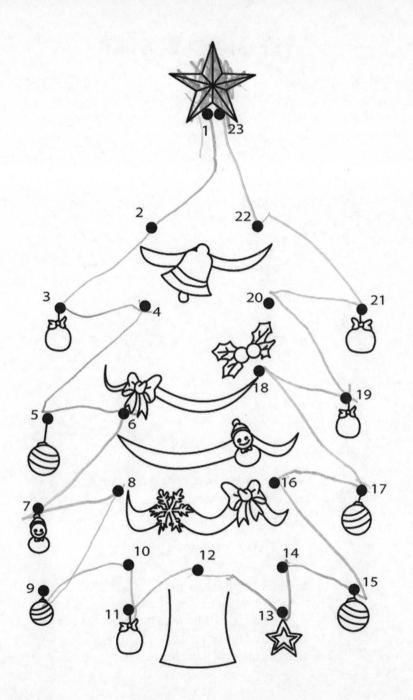

THE ANGELS' SONG

G O O D W I L L T O M E N

ACROSS

5. The shepherds take care of the _____.
6. The angels were called the _____ host.
7. The angels sang _____ to God.

DOWN

1. The sheep are cared for by the _____.
2. The angels brought tidings of great _____.
3. The _____ of the Lord shone round about the angels.
4. The angels told the shepherds to _____.
6. The angels were called the heavenly _____.

READING WRITING ARITHMETIC

Fill in the missing letters, and the circled letters will form a word or phrase from top to bottom.

◯CISSORS

PEN◯IL

TEAC◯ER

B◯OKS

N◯TEBOOKS

G◯UE

◯ESKS

ER◯SERS

CRA◯ONS

BU◯

The Christ Child

Can you answer these questions about the Christ Child?

Long before Jesus was born, God gave Him many titles.
Can you name any of them hidden in Isaiah 9:6?

_____

_____

_____

_____

_____

When will God's Kingdom end? The answer is hidden in Isaiah 9:7.

_____

Winter Holiday
New Year

```
M  T  F  C  E  L  T  P
I  G  P  O  X  L  G  K
D  J  A  N  U  A  R  Y
N  P  R  F  H  B  N  E
I  O  T  E  A  Z  M  A
G  L  I  T  T  E  R  R
H  A  E  T  S  N  E  W
T  S  S  I  K  G  S  T
```

glitter	confetti	hats
ball	January	midnight
kiss	parties	new
	year	

GIFT MAGIC

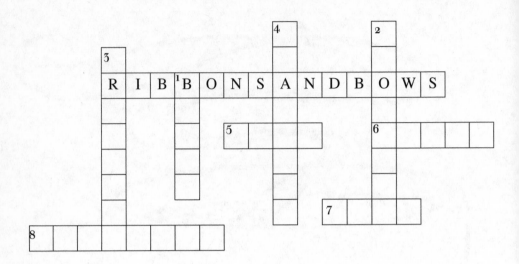

ACROSS

5. This sticky stuff keeps the paper in place.
6. What we wrap the presents in.
7. We write names on these and stick them to the presents.
8. We use these to cut the paper to the right size.

DOWN

1. We put the gifts in these before we wrap them.
2. Before we can wrap the presents, we have to go _____.
3. Another word for gifts.
4. We use this kind of paper.

SOUND SLEEPERS

Fill in the missing letters, and the circled letters will form a word or phrase from top to bottom.

C◯IPMUNKS

AN◯MALS

◯EARS

CAV◯S

BEA◯S

S◯AILS

B◯TS

◯URTLES

SLEEP◯NG

W◯ODCHUCKS

S◯AKES

PICTURE THIS

Draw a line from each picture to its matching word in the middle. When you are through, a few words will be left over. Fill them in on the lines below to form a phrase.

silent

ornaments

stocking

night

toys

present

_____ _____

WHAT DO YOU KNOW?

The Three Kings

Can you answer these questions about the three kings who came to visit the Christ Child?

These kings came to Jerusalem from far away in the East. How did they find their way? The answer is hidden in Matthew 2:2.

_____

What did the three kings do when they found Jesus? The answer is hidden in Matthew 2:11.

_____

What gifts did the three kings bring to Jesus? The answer is hidden in Matthew 2:11.

_____

Winter Holiday
Thanksgiving

```
W  I  S  H  B  O  N  E
L  N  L  Y  V  A  R  G
O  T  A  T  O  P  E  W
K  U  J  G  J  P  N  I
D  R  E  S  S  I  N  G
V  K  R  L  R  E  I  R
B  E  A  N  S  S  D  Y
W  Y  L  I  M  A  F  M
```

turkey	dressing	gravy
pies	wishbone	dinner
family	potato	beans

89

HOLIDAY CHEER

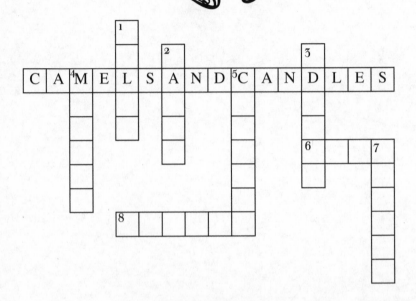

C A M E L S A N D C A N D L E S

ACROSS

6. The First _____

8. The songs we sing at Christmas are called _____.

DOWN

1. We like to ring these at Christmas.

2. We sign and send these to our friends at Christmas.

3. A time of prayer during the holidays.

4. Mary laid Jesus in a _____ bed.

5. We love to bake all kinds of these at Christmas.

7. We wrap these around the tree and turn them on.

WINTER WEATHER TERMS

Fill in the missing letters, and the circled letters will form a word or phrase from top to bottom.

H◯IL

FLU◯RIES

I◯E

S◯ORM

W◯NDCHILL

◯LOUDY

◯ROST

F◯EEZE

C◯LD

S◯OWFALL

SLEE◯

PICTURE THIS

Draw a line from each picture to its matching word in the middle. When you are through, a few words will be left over. Fill them in on the lines below to form a phrase.

camel

bells

Mary

and

Joseph

baby Jesus

angel

_____ ___ _____

HOLIDAY SONGS

Find the missing words from the list below.

IT'S BEGINNING TO _____ A LOT LIKE CHRISTMAS

I _____ THE BELLS ON CHRISTMAS DAY

LITTLE _____ BOY

_____ NAVIDAD

O _____ TREE

DRUMMER   FELIZ   CHRISTMAS

HEARD   LOOK

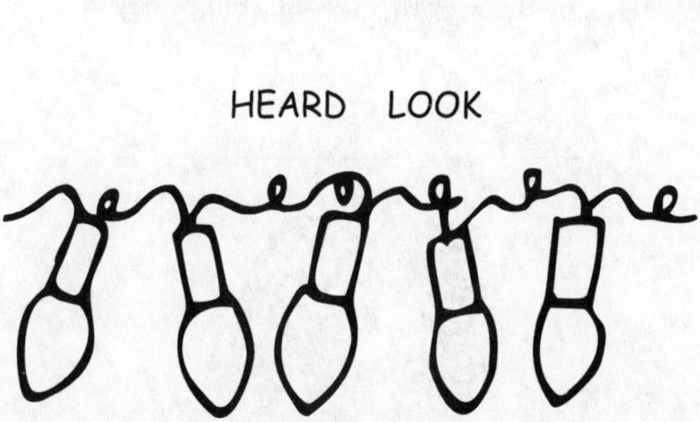

WHAT DO YOU KNOW?

Winter in the Bible

The Bible has a lot to say about wintertime.
Can you answer these questions?

What is as refreshing as a faithful messenger? The answer is hidden in Isaiah 55:13.

_____

What is it like when someone promises you a gift but doesn't give it to you? The answer is hidden in Proverbs 25:14.

_____

What is it like when you sing a cheerful song to someone who is sad? The answer is hidden in Isaiah 55:20.

_____

Winter Holiday
Christmas

```
F G I F T S W C
I N O R T H P A
R E I N D E E R
T S E V L E K O
R S L E I G H L
E T O B E L L S
E A P A T N A R
O R N A M E N T
```

gifts	reindeer	ornament
North	sleigh	elves
Pole	fir tree	bells
	star	carols

96

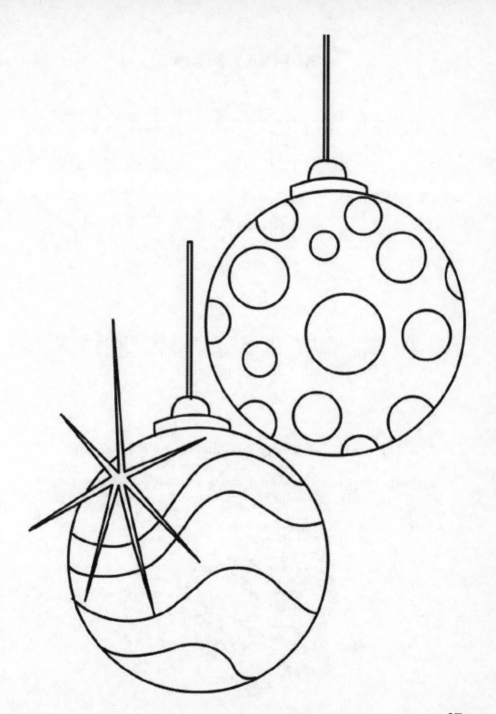

HOLIDAY PIES

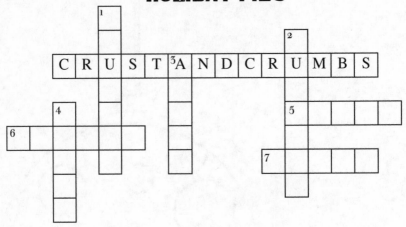

C	R	U	S	T	³A	N	D	C	R	U	M	B	S

ACROSS

5. This is a nutty pie we like to make at Thanksgiving.
6. This pie is made with small, tart, red fruit.
7. This pie sometimes has the word "meat" in it.

DOWN

1. This pie is made from a stalk that grows in the north.
2. This pie is made from a big, orange gourd.
3. This pie is made from round, red fruit. It's the American pie.
4. This pie has fluffy, white meringue on top.

98

PILED HIGH

Fill in the missing letters, and the circled letters will form a word or phrase from top to bottom.

SAN◯

FLURR◯ES

STREN◯TH

FRI◯ID

DR◯FTS

I◯CHES

◯LOVES

SH◯VEL

SL◯SH

BOO◯S

WHAT DO YOU KNOW?

Winter in the Bible

The Bible has a lot to say about wintertime. Can you answer these questions?

The Bible says that the "coming of refreshing rain in winter" is like what? The answer is hidden in Hosea 6:3.

_____

The Bible says the "cold" comes from where? The answer is hidden in Job 37:9.

_____

The Bible says "ice" comes from where?
The answer is hidden in Job 37:10.

_____

Winter Sports

```
S L E D D I N G
K H L O R S E N
A O F M A D T I
T C R G O E A I
I K A L B E K K
N E J U M P S S
G Y N G Z S E W
S H O E S B L X
```

skating	jumps	hockey
sledding	board	shoes
luge	skiing	speed
	skate	

T

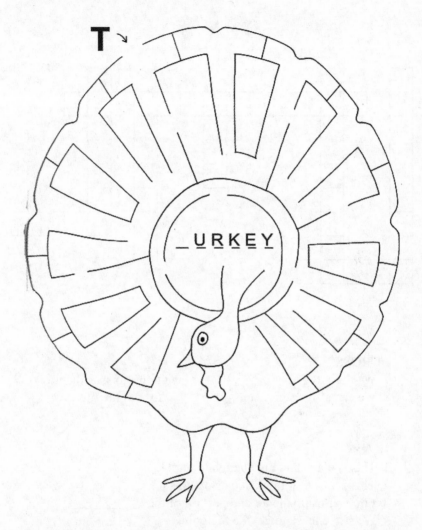

_ U R K E Y

Help "T" to find the rest of his word. . .TURKEY.

WINTER SIGHTS

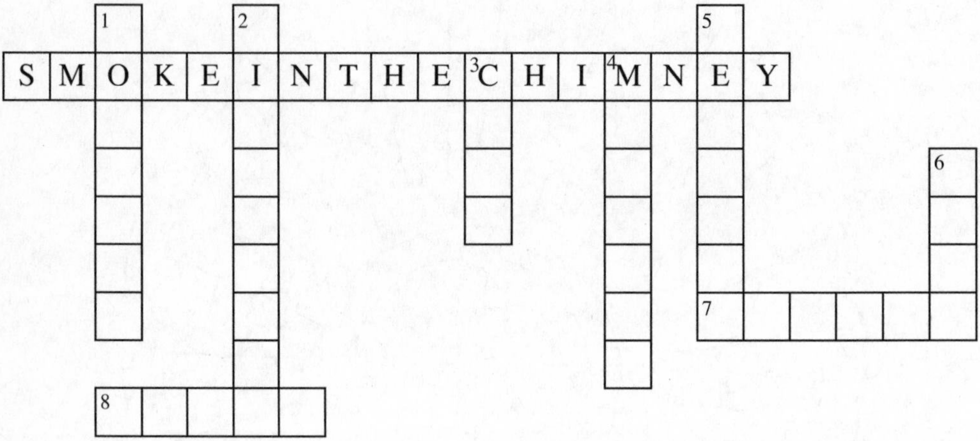
SMOKE IN THE CHIMNEY

ACROSS

7. We need to gather up __________ and twigs to start the fire.
8. We can also crumple up __________ to start the fire.

DOWN

1. This is black and big enough to burn logs.
2. This is made of brick and also burns logs.
3. Fire warms up the air and gets rid of the __________.
4. We strike these to get the fire going.
5. We can also use electric _________ to warm up the room.
6. We chop the wood into ____________.

MARYS MIRACLE

Fill in the missing letters, and the circled letters will form a word or phrase from top to bottom.

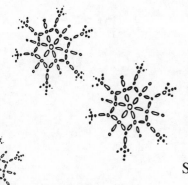

JE◯US

NAT◯VITY

ANGE◯S

SHEPH◯RDS

DO◯KEY

S◯AR

A◯IMALS

K◯NG OF KINGS

MAN◯ER

JOSEP◯

BIR◯H

PICTURE THIS

Draw a line from each picture to its matching word in the middle. When you are through, a few words will be left over. Fill them in on the lines below to form a phrase.

pie

stocking

a

manger

lamb

winter weather

bed

___ _____ ____ _____

HOLIDAY SONGS

Find the missing words from the list below.

HAVE YOURSELF A _____ LITTLE CHRISTMAS

_____ WE HAVE HEARD ON HIGH

GOD _____ YE MERRY GENTLEMEN

O COME ALL YE _____

THE _____ NOEL

FIRST   REST   FAITHFUL

MERRY   ANGELS

WHAT DO YOU KNOW?

Winter in the Bible

The apostle Paul was arrested and sent to Rome on a ship where he would be put on trial. High winds and winter storms made the trip very dangerous. Can you answer these questions about Paul's winter journey?

Where did the ship finally stop?
The answer is hidden in Acts 27:7–8.

_____

When they left Fair Havens, Paul's ship set sail for what harbor in Crete? The answer is hidden in Acts 27:12.

_____

Everyone was afraid when the ship started to sink. What did Paul tell the frightened men who were on the ship with him? The answer is hidden in Acts 27:22.

_____

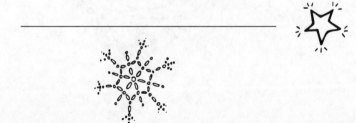

Winter Months

```
A P R I L W M R
L K F L A G E S
Y R A U R B E F
D E C E M B E R
C B A E O D Y O
P R V H C R A M
L O C T O B E R
N Y R A U N A J
```

October   December   February

November   January   March

April

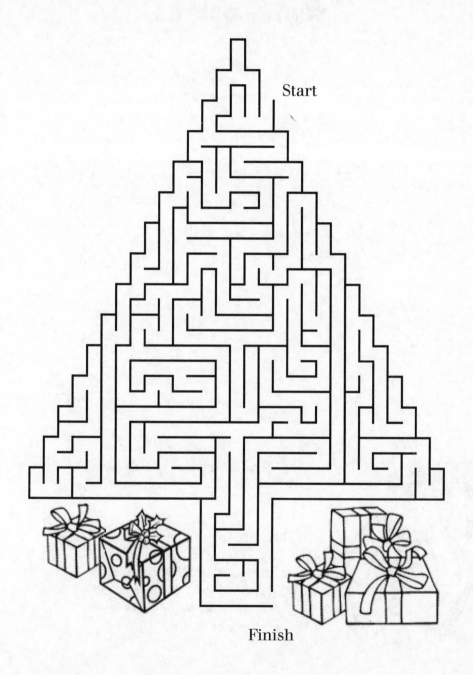

Start

Finish

WINTER MONTHS

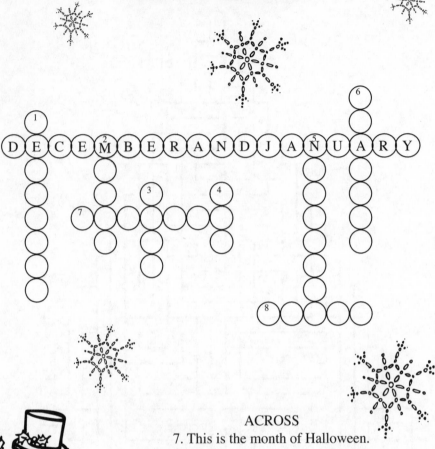

The crossword puzzle shows: DECEMBER AND JANUARY

ACROSS
7. This is the month of Halloween.
8. This month's showers wash the snow away.

DOWN
1. This is the second month of the new year.
2. This is the last month of winter.
3. The winter months are not hot; they are _____.
4. When we're cold we make this sound.
5. This is the month of Thanksgiving.
6. Winter is one of the four _____.

114

JOSEPHS JOURNEY

Fill in the missing letters, and the circled letters will form a word or phrase from top to bottom.

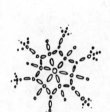

__ A G I

__ G Y P T

H E __ O D

N O __ O O M

D O N K E __

C H R I S T __ H I L D

S __ E P H E R D S

M A __ Y

B __ R T H

A N G E L __

S __ A R

E __ M A N U E L

N __ T I V I T Y

J E __ U S

PICTURE THIS

Draw a line from each picture to its matching word in the middle. When you are through, a few words will be left over. Fill them in on the lines below to form a phrase.

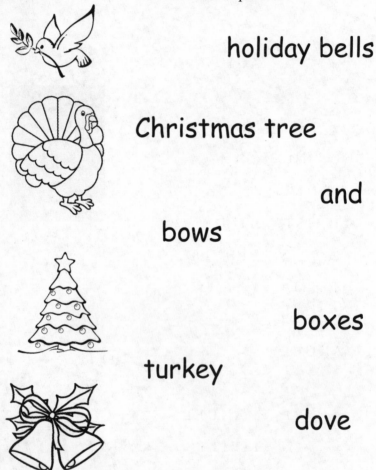

holiday bells

Christmas tree

and

bows

boxes

turkey

dove

_____ __ ____

HOLIDAY STORIES

Find the missing words from the list below.

THE _____ MATCH GIRL

'TWAS THE _____ BEFORE CHRISTMAS

CHRISTMAS AT THE _____

THE _____ AND THE SHOEMAKER

THE COBBLER'S _____

ELVES   QUEST   CRATCHITS

LITTLE   NIGHT

WHAT DO YOU KNOW?

Winter in the Bible

The wind can be very cold in the wintertime. Can you answer these questions about the wind?

When the winter winds and rain beat against the house built on the rock, did it fall or did it stand strong? The answer is hidden in Matthew 7:25.

_____

When the tall waves and winter wind started to sink the boat Jesus and His disciples were sailing in, Jesus stood up and spoke to the storm. What did Jesus say? The answer is hidden in Mark 4:37–39.

_____

Where does the Bible say that God walks? The answer is hidden in Psalm 104:3.

_____

The Worst of Winter

```
B L U S T E R Y
G N I Z E E R F
I C E S T O R M
T H C H I L L W
E O U C O L D I
E B L E A K C N
L K F R I G I D
S N I F F L E S
```

blustery	freezing	ice storm
cold	bleak	sniffles
sleet	chill	winds
frigid	flu	

SIGNS OF SPRING

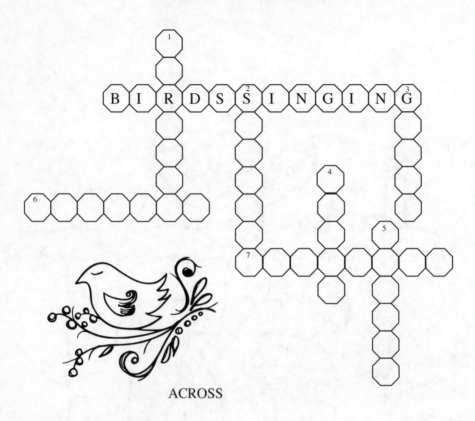

ACROSS

6. We love to stop and smell the beautiful _____.
7. We love to feel the _____ on our faces.

DOWN

1. Instead of cold air, we have _____.
2. The spring _____ wash away the snow.
3. In the spring, the grass turns _____.
4. Get out the lawn mower, it's time to cut the _____.
5. We sit on the green grass and have a _____.

THE CHRISTMAS STORY

Fill in the missing letters, and the letters will form a word or phrase from top to bottom.

C _ RIST

H _ AVENLY

K _ NG

CRO _ S

DI _

REDEE _ ER

PRO _ ISES

S _ VIOR

SI _ LESS

SO _ L

J _ SUS

_ AMB OF GOD

PICTURE THIS

Draw a line from each picture to its matching word in the middle. When you are through, a few words will be left over. Fill them in on the lines below to form a phrase.

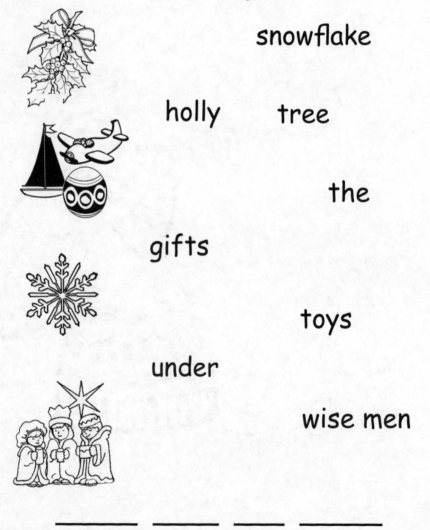

snowflake

holly   tree

the

gifts

toys

under

wise men

_____ _____ _____ _____

WHAT DO YOU KNOW?

Winter in the Bible

The Bible has a lot to say about wintertime.
Can you answer these questions?

The Bible names five kinds of "weather." Can you name them? The answer is hidden in Psalm 148:8.

_____

_____

_____

_____

_____

What did all these types of weather do? The answer is hidden in Psalm 148:8.

_____

Winter's End

```
W A R M A I R K
U R A E F S U N
S T I L L E S U
M S N T O T E N
O D K I W K E E
O U D N E G R E
L B E G R H T R
B I R D S O N G
```

green	warm air	buds
flowers	melting	sun
blooms	birdsong	rain
	trees	

128

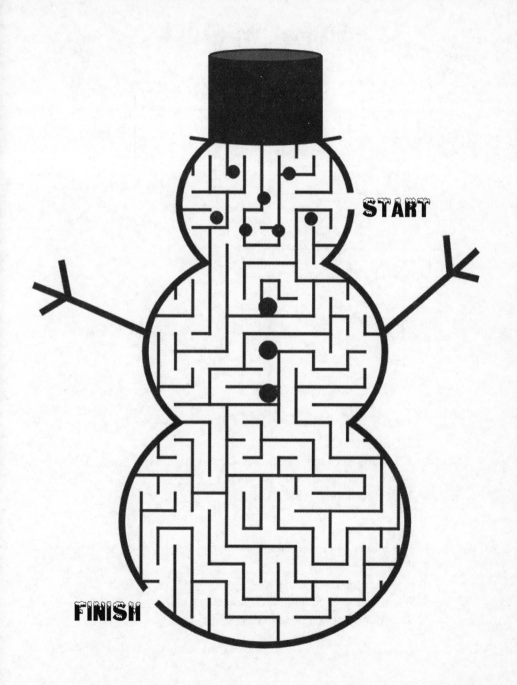

START

FINISH

STORMY WEATHER

| W | I | N | T | E | R | W | H | I | T | E | O | U | T |

ACROSS

6. When the trees and the clouds are moving, it's _____.
7. A really bad snowstorm is called a _____.
8. Water from the clouds is called _____.

DOWN

1. The snow piles up and makes _____.
2. Winter winds blow in _____ air.
3. In winter the roads can get _____.
4. When rain freezes into hard chunks, we call it _____.
5. Stormy weather can be very _____.

WHO IS THAT MAN?

Fill in the missing letters, and the letters will form a word or phrase
from top to bottom.

__ U S T

H __ A L E R

M E __ S I A H

P __ R E

C H R I __ T

__ A V I O R

L __ V E

S I __ L E S S

H __ L Y

__ R I E N D

K I N __

L __ R D

R E __ __ E E M E R

PICTURE THIS

Draw a line from each picture to its matching word in the middle. When you are through, a few words will be left over. Fill them in on the lines below to form a phrase.

candy cane

the   stocking

shoppers

drummer

boy   holly

_____ _____ _____

WHAT DO YOU KNOW?

Winter in the Bible

The Bible uses snow to describe the whitest white of all. Can you answer these questions about things that are "as white as snow"?

What does the Bible say was "white as snow"? The answer is hidden in Daniel 7:9.

_____

What does the Bible say shall be as "white as snow"? The answer is hidden in Isaiah 1:18.

_____

What does the Bible say God will do to make us "whiter than snow"? The answer is hidden in Psalm 51:7.

_____

Groundhog Day

```
F O R E C A S T
E L W A T C H C
B K S L P N A I
R E T N I W D D
U D A Y S L O E
A B U R R O W R
R G N I R P S P
Y W E A T H E R
```

burrow	spring	shadow
predict	weather	forecast
winter	watch	February

FAMILY FUN

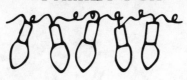

| T | R | I | M | M | I | N | G | T | H | E | T | R | E | E |

ACROSS

6. Striped candy with a hook, these are candy _____.
7. There are jingle _____ and silver _____.
8. These are made with brightly colored ribbon.

DOWN

1. This goes on top of the tree.
2. These are shiny strips of paper to brighten the tree.
3. These comes in all colors and flash off and on.
4. These are under the tree to be opened on Christmas Day.
5. These come in many shapes, colors, and sizes.

138

REINDEER TRACKS

Fill in the missing letters to form a word or phrase from top to bottom.

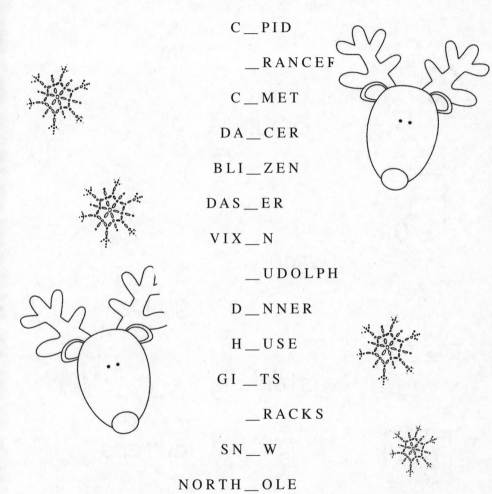

C _ P I D

_ R A N C E R

C _ M E T

D A _ _ C E R

B L I _ Z E N

D A S _ E R

V I X _ N

_ U D O L P H

D _ N N E R

H _ U S E

G I _ T S

_ R A C K S

S N _ _ W

N O R T H _ O L E

PICTURE THIS

Draw a line from each picture to its matching word in the middle. When you are through, a few words will be left over. Fill them in on the lines below to form a phrase.

drum

candle

the

wrap

gifts

stocking

mittens

_____ _____ _____

HOLIDAY STORIES

Find the missing words from the list below.

MRS BROWNLOWS' CHRISTMAS _____

HARRY, THE SINGING _____

NO CRIB FOR A _____

THE GIFT OF THE _____

A CHRISTMAS _____ AND HOW IT CAME TRUE

ANGEL   BED   DREAM

MAGI   PARTY

WHAT DO YOU KNOW?

Winter in the Bible

The Bible has a lot to say about wintertime. Can you answer these questions?

The Bible says the "snow" is like what?
The answer is hidden in Psalm 147:16.

_____

In the same psalm, the Bible says the "frost" is like what?
The answer is hidden in Psalm 147:16.

_____

What is it God says to the "snow"? The answer is hidden in Job 37:6.

_____

Winter Birds

B L A C K A R T

B I R D S B O H

L F E T P L B R

U I V S A U I U

E N O W R E N S

J C D A R T L H

A H W M O I F E

Y S R R W W T O S

black	wrens	robin
bird	finch	bluetit
bluejay	thrushes	sparrow
	dove	

143

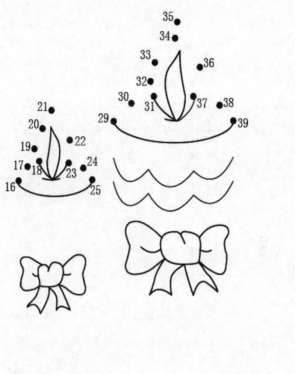

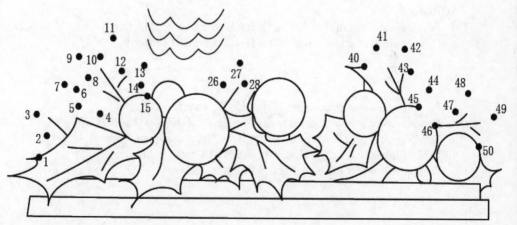

PRESIDENTS DAY REVIEW

| A | M | E | R | I | C | A | N | P | R | E | S | I | D | E | N | T | S |

ACROSS

6. This president's name sounds like a car. His first name is Gerald.
7. This president resigned from office. His first name is Richard.

DOWN

1. This president was once a movie star. His first name was Ronald.
2. This president's wife might also run for president. His first name is Bill.
3. This president once lived on a peanut farm. His first name is Jimmy.
4. This president was called Honest Abe. His first name is Abraham.
5. This president was the first. His first name is George.

147

PICTURE THIS

Draw a line from each picture to its matching word in the middle. When you are through, a few words will be left over. Fill them in on the lines below to form a phrase.

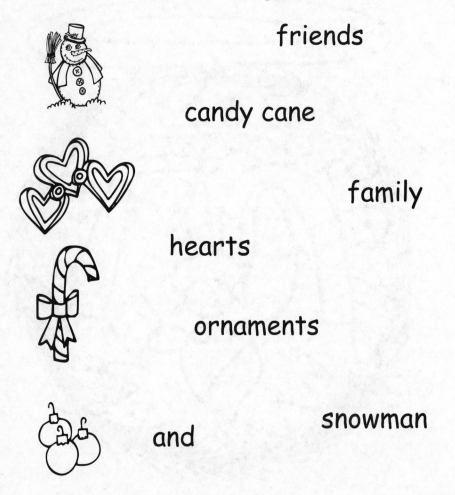

friends

candy cane

family

hearts

ornaments

snowman

and

_____ _____ _____

HOLIDAY GREETINGS

Find the missing words from the list below.

CHRISTMAS IS FOR _____

THE CHRISTMAS _____ IS A GIVING HEART

GOOD _____ OF GREAT JOY

JESUS IS THE _____ FOR THE SEASON

THE JOY OF CHRISTMAS BRINGS US _____ TO EACH OTHER

GOD _____ US EVERYONE

BLESS   TIDINGS CLOSER

HEART   CHILDREN   REASON

WHAT DO YOU KNOW?

Winter in the Bible

The Bible says that God is the only one who can control the weather. He decides when it will be cold and when it will be warm. Can you answer these questions?

What does the Bible say only God can do? The answer is hidden in Job 37:3.

_____

What does the Bible say only God can call down from heaven? The answer is hidden in Job 37:6.

_____

What is it the Bible says God's people are safe from even when this kind of weather comes down on them? The answer is hidden in Isaiah 32:18–19.

_____

The Best of Winter

```
S  N  E  L  O  O  W  D
C  S  E  I  K  S  P  S
A  O  C  O  C  T  O  H
R  G  O  N  G  G  E  O
F  S  D  E  L  S  D  A
S  K  A  T  E  S  K  L
S  W  E  A  T  E  R  S
W  A  R  M  F  I  R  E
```

warm fire	scarfs	skies
woolens	sweaters	sleds
hot cocoa	skates	eggnog

FINISH

GROUNDHOG DAY

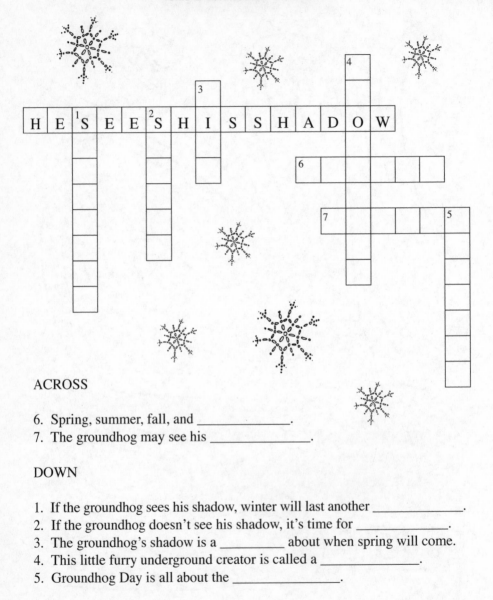

ACROSS

6. Spring, summer, fall, and _____.
7. The groundhog may see his _____.

DOWN

1. If the groundhog sees his shadow, winter will last another _____.
2. If the groundhog doesn't see his shadow, it's time for _____.
3. The groundhog's shadow is a _____ about when spring will come.
4. This little furry underground creator is called a _____.
5. Groundhog Day is all about the _____.

PLAYING IN THE SNOW

Fill in the missing letters to form a word or phrase from top to bottom.

__ U N

CO __ N C O B   P I P E

B U T T __ N

N O __ E

T H U M P I __ Y

E __ E S

S __ O P

__ U R R I E D

S T R __ E T S

__ N O W

R U __ N I N G

C __ A L

__ A V E D

B R O O __ S T I C K

H __ N D

B R A __ C H

WHAT DO YOU KNOW?

Winter in the Bible

The wind and weather are no problem for God. Can you answer these questions?

What does the Bible say God rode on when He flew upon the wings of the wind? The answer is hidden in Psalm 18:10.

_____

The Bible says that dark waters and what other kind of weather was round about God? The answer is hidden in Psalm 18:11.

_____

What does the Bible say God did in the heavens?
The answer is hidden in Psalm 18:13.

_____

Journey of the Magi!

```
T  S  A  E  Z  Y  S  O
H  R  R  Y  M  R  T  S
R  E  M  N  D  O  A  T
E  M  R  S  Y  L  R  F
E  D  L  U  G  G  O  I
Y  B  A  B  D  N  A  G
S  L  E  M  A  C  I  O
S  T  A  B  L  E  M  K
```

camels   baby   gold
three   east   stable
kings   myrrh   gifts
       star

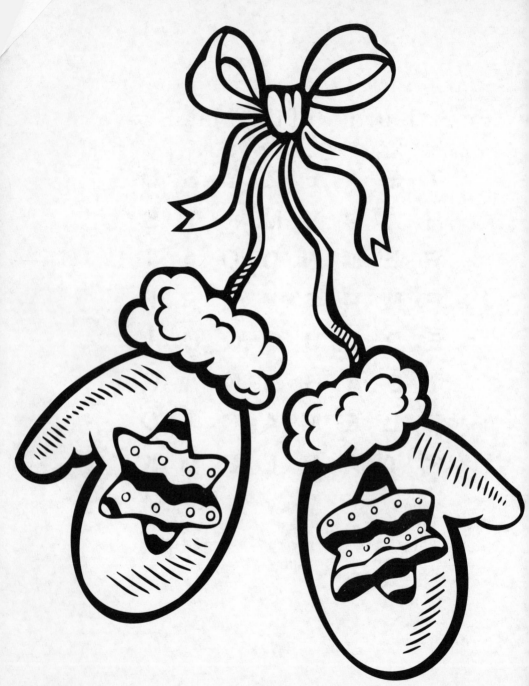

START

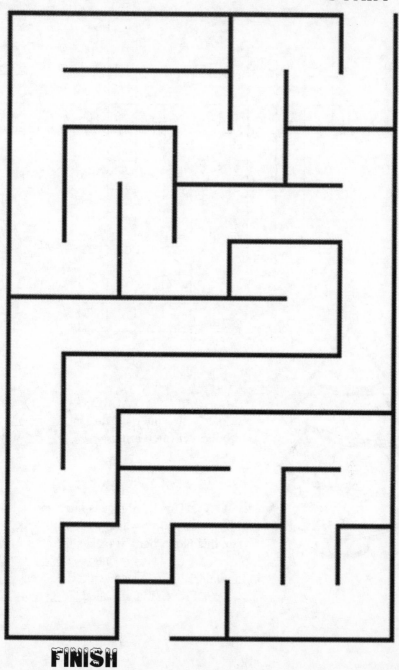

FINISH

161

WINTER BLAST

S	H	I	V	E	R	A	N	D	S	H	A	K	E

ACROSS

7. In winter, the air is _____.
8. Winter often brings _____ weather.

DOWN

1. This word means intensely cold.
2. When water hardens into ice.
3. When this blows hard, it makes the air seem even colde
4. A very noisy wind is _____.
5. In winter, the streets and sidewalks get _____.
6. Frozen rain is called _____.

162

KINGLY GIFTS

Fill in the missing letters to form a word or phrase from top to bottom.

P _ _ A Y

K _ _ N G

B E _ _ H L E H E M

G I F _ _ S

S M I _ _ E D

B _ _ S T

_ _ R U M

H O N O _ _

P A R _ _ M

P U _ _ P U M

_ _ A G I

J _ _ S U S

P _ _ A I S E

L A M _ _

S _ _ N G

B A B _ _

PICTURE THIS

Draw a line from each picture to its matching word in the middle. When you are through, a few words will be left over. Fill them in on the lines below to form a phrase.

Christmas tree

no

snowman

the

inn

star

teddy bear

room

in

_____ _____ _____ _____ _____

WHAT DO YOU KNOW?

Winter in the Bible

The Bible has a lot to say about wintertime.
Can you answer these questions?

Where do the "snow and rain" come from? The answer is hidden in Isaiah 55:10.

_____

How do the "rain and snow" make the earth better? The answer is hidden in Isaiah 55:10.

_____

_____

_____

What does the Bible say is like the "rain and snow"? The answer is hidden in Isaiah 55:11.

_____

ANSWERS

7

Taste of the Holidays

C	O	O	K	I	E	S	A
G	H	C	N	U	P	W	Z
N	B	E	R	R	I	E	S
I	N	A	R	C	H	E	W
D	R	P	O	T	A	T	O
D	P	L	N	B	M	A	K
U	I	U	C	A	K	E	I
P	E	M	T	I	U	R	F

cookies berries ham
plum sweet pie
pudding potato fruit
crab cake

7

9

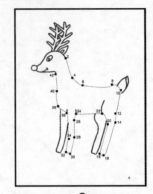

9

10

COOKIE TIME

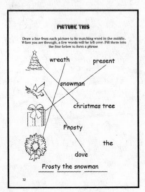

ACROSS

1. Christmas is a great time to bake _____
4. This cookie is made with cinnamon and nutmeg
6. This cookie smells like a sandwich with jam
7. This is a cereal cookie with oats and raisins

DOWN

1. This is what you use to shape the cookie dough
2. You might sprinkle some of these on your cookie dough
3. This cookie is made from a duck, starky syrup
5. This cookie is extra sweet and cut into shapes

10

11

WINTER WARM UPS

Fill in the missing letters to form a word or phrase from top to bottom.

HOTCH(O)COLATE
WA(S)SAIL
CA(P)S
FIRE(P)LACE
FAMIL(Y)
(H)EATERS
GL(O)VES
B(L)ANKET
M(I)TTENS
WOO(L)
CO(A)TS
(O)Y
(S)WEATERS

11

12

PICTURE THIS

Draw a line from each picture to its matching word in the middle. When you are through, a few words will be left over. Fill them into the line below to form a phrase

wreath   present

snowman

christmas tree

Frosty

the

dove

Frosty the snowman

12

13

HOLIDAY SONGS

Find the missing word from the list below and finish the sentence.

SILENT NIGHT

DO YOU HEAR WHAT I HEAR?

JINGLE BELLS ROCK

I'M DREAMING OF A WHITE CHRISTMAS

WE THREE KINGS

HEAR DREAMING ROCK
NIGHT THREE

13

Page 14

WHAT DO YOU KNOW?
A Girl Named Mary

Mary was not just any young woman. God chose her to be the mother of the Christ Child. When God spoke to her, she was willing to do whatever He asked of her. Can you answer these questions?

Who did God send to Galilee to speak to Mary about the baby she would be having? The answer is hidden in Luke 1:26.

The angel Gabriel

Who was Mary engaged to when the angel spoke to her? The answer is hidden in Luke 1:27.

Joseph

Who was the father of Joseph, the husband of Mary, who was Jesus' mother. The answer is hidden in Matthew 1:16.

Jesus

The angel also told Mary to name her son Jesus, but He would also be called what? The answer is hidden in Luke 1:35.

The Son of God

Page 15

Winter Weather

N	O	S	C	H	O	O	L
S	E	L	C	I	C	I	G
W	F	E	S	N	O	W	L
I	C	E	S	T	A	H	O
N	O	T	M	Q	T	Y	V
D	L	S	Y	A	S	L	E
R	D	P	B	O	O	T	S
W	S	N	E	T	T	I	M

snow	icicles	gloves
ice	cold	coats
sleet	boots	mittens
no school	hats	wind

Page 17

Start

Finish

Page 19

FEBRUARY FORECASTER

Fill in the missing letters to focus a word or phrase from top to bottom.

UNDER G ROUND

BUR R OW

R O DENT

CLO U DY

SU N NY

PRE D ICTION

WEAT H ER

SHAD O W

EARLYSPRIN G

WOO D CHUCK

HOLID A Y

M Y TH

Page 20

PICTURE THIS

Draw a line from each picture to its matching word in the middle. When you are through, a few words will be left over. Fill them into the line below to form a phrase.

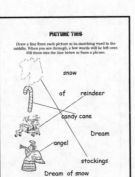

snow

of   reindeer

candy cane

Dream

angel

stockings

Dream of snow _____

Page 21

HOLIDAY SONGS

Find the missing word from the list below and finish the sentence

WINTER WONDERLAND

GOOD KING WENSELAS

AWAY IN A MANGER

HAPPY HOLIDAYS TO YOU

WHILE SHEPHERDS WATCHED THEIR FLOCKS

MANGER HOLIDAYS KING
SHEPHERDS WONDERLAND

Page 22

WHAT DO YOU KNOW?

Jesus Is Born

When Jesus was born, Mary and Joseph were not at their home or even in their own city. Can you answer these questions about their journey to Bethlehem?

What powerful king said that everyone had to be registered in the cities where they were born? The answer is hidden in Luke 2:1.

Caesar Augustus

Mary and Joseph went to Bethlehem because Joseph was a descendant of what great king?
The answer is hidden in
Luke 2:4

King David

Mary had her baby while they were on their trip. Why did she wrap up her new baby and lay Him in a manger filled with hay?
The answer is hidden in Luke 2:7.

There wasn't any room so they had to stay in the barn or stable.

22

Page 23

Winter Games

S	N	O	W	M	A	N	S
S	K	A	T	I	N	G	D
W	L	R	Y	L	E	L	F
D	E	L	S	D	M	P	I
K	G	D	F	G	G	Q	G
M	N	Y	E	K	C	O	H
N	A	G	G	O	B	O	T
L	L	A	B	W	O	N	S

snowman   angel   snowball
skating   sled   fights
hockey   toboggan

23

Page 25

25

Page 26

THANKSGIVING DINNER

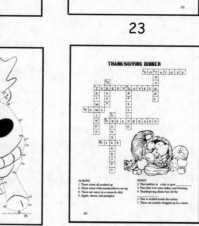

ACROSS
1. These items all mashed up
8. These come with marshmallows on top
8. There are many in a casserole dish
9. Apple, cherry, and pumpkin

DOWN
2. This holiday is a day to give ____
3. Pour this over your turkey and dressing
4. Thanksgiving dinner has all the

A. This is stuffed inside the turkey
7. These are usually chopped up in a sauce

26

Page 27

NIP IN THE AIR

Fill in the missing letters to form a word or phrase from top to bottom.

LONG **J** OHNS

E **A** RMUFFS

HOT **C** HOCOLATE

JAC **K** ET

MU **F** FLER

BLUSTER **Y**

C **O** LDSNAP

BRIS **K**

MIT **T** ENS

27

Page 28

PICTURE THIS

Draw a line from each picture to its matching word in the middle. When you are through, a few words will be left over. Fill them into the line below to form a phrase.

mistletoe

Under

christmas tree

baby Jesus

candle

bells

the

Under the mistletoe

28

29

THANKSGIVING SONGS

Find the missing word from the list below and finish the sentence

NOW THANK WE ALL OUR **GOD**

COME, YE THANKFUL PEOPLE COME!

WE GATHER **BLESSINGS**

WITH THANKFUL HEARTS, O LORD WE COME

COUNT YOUR **BLESSINGS**

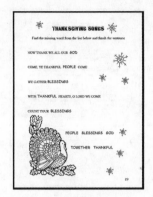

PEOPLE   BLESSINGS   GOD

TOGETHER   THANKFUL

30

WHAT DO YOU KNOW?

The Shepherds Joy

On the night Jesus, the Christ Child, was born, some shepherds were up in the hills taking care of their sheep. All of a sudden, the sky lit up. Can you answer these questions?

Who appeared in the sky and told them not to be afraid?
The answer is hidden in Luke 2:9.

An angel of the Lord

The angel told the shepherds that a baby had been born. What did the angel call the baby? The answer is hidden in Luke 2:11.

A Savior, who is Christ the Lord.

The angels told the shepherds where they could find the baby Jesus. Where did they say He would be lying?
The answer is hidden in Luke 2:12.

Lying in a manger.

31

Holiday Treats!

```
C O O K I E S P
A I P E A N U T
N R D A M S G C
D I W E G E A A
Y B A L R F R N
O B R I T T L E
W O G O N G G E
G N I K C O T S
```

candy   sugar   stocking
cane   cookies   peanut
ribbon   eggnog   brittle
                              cider

33

34

WINTER FUN

ACROSS
3. In the winter, the air is _____
5. When snow comes a light twinkle, the weatherman calls it _____
8. When the wind blows hard, we say it's _____

DOWN
1. White, fluffy stuff that falls from the sky
2. There are called stones but they are really balls of frozen rain
3. This makes pretty patterns on the windows
5. These sparkly things hang from the tree branches and rooftops
6. When it's really cold outside, we say it's _____

35

FUN FUN FUN

Fill in the missing letters to form a word or phrase from top to bottom.

NORTH **W** IND
IC **E**
FL **U** RRIES
C **O** LD
GL **O** VES
M **I** TTENS
SL **E** IGHRIDES
W OOLENS
SKI **I** NG
S **N** OWBALLS
CHRIS **T** MAS
B **E** AUTY
F **R** OST

PICTURE THIS

Draw a line from each picture to its matching word in the middle. When you are through, a few words will be left over. Fill them into the line below to form a phrase.

mittens

Turkey

christmas tree

day

sledding

fun

harvest

Turkey fun day

36

Herod's Evil Plan

When King Herod heard that some kings from the East were looking for the Christ Child, he was angry and disturbed. Can you answer these questions?

Who did Herod call on to tell him about the Christ Child? The answer is hidden in Matthew 2:4.

_____

Where was the Christ Child born?

What did these advisors tell King Herod about where the Christ Child would be born? The answer is hidden in Matthew 2:5.

Bethlehem

_____

What did the advisors tell King Herod about what the Christ Child would do? The answer is hidden in Matthew 2:6.

Shepherd Israel

_____

38

All About Ice___

S	O	S	E	T	A	K	S
C	A	P	M	A	E	R	C
R	E	N	Y	W	S	T	R
A	L	B	E	R	G	T	Y
P	C	E	K	L	O	M	S
E	I	I	C	Y	X	Y	T
R	C	F	O	B	A	N	A
F	I	S	H	I	N	G	L

berg   hockey   ice
cap   scraper   icicle
crystal   skates   steam
fishing

39

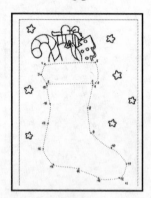

41

SALUTE TO WINTER

WINTERTIMEWONDER
SKATES
HOCKEY

ACROSS
7. A game played with sticks on the ice
8. What the sun forms a lioness

DOWN
1. We ride these down the hills
2. These are pieces of wood we attach to our feet
3. These are made by rolling the snow into big balls
4. Snow, water, cold, and wind are all kinds of _____
5. We can glide over the ice with these on our feet
6. We can't see this, but we feel it when it blows

42

THE GREAT OUTDOORS

SNOWSHOE

SKIING

SNOWMAN

SNOWSHOE

SKIING

SNOWMAN

SKATING

ICEFISHING

CROSSCOUNTRY

SLEDDING

SKIJUMP

HOCKEY

SNOWBOARD

HUNTING

43

PICTURE THIS

Draw a line from each picture to its matching word in the middle. When you are through, a few words will be left over. Fill them onto the line below to form a phrase.

stocking

present

Light

the

tree

nutcracker

Christmas

gingerbread man

Light the Christmas tree

44

HOLIDAY SONGS

Find the missing word from the list below and finish the sentence.

TWELVE DAYS OF CHRISTMAS

SILVER BELLS

ROCKIN' AROUND THE CHRISTMAS TREE

WHITE CHRISTMAS

THERE'S NO PLACE LIKE HOME FOR THE HOLIDAYS

TREE   CHRISTMAS   HOME

TWELVE   BELLS

45

WHAT DO YOU KNOW?

Naming the Baby

Mary and Joseph did everything they could for their new baby. Can you answer these questions?

When Jesus was eight days old, what did His parents name Him? The answer is hidden in Luke 2:21.

They named Him Jesus.

Where did Mary and Joseph take their new son a few days later? The answer is hidden in Luke 2:22.

They went to Jerusalem to present Jesus to the Lord.

What else did Mary and Joseph do while they were in Jerusalem? The answer is hidden in Luke 2:24.

They offered a sacrifice.

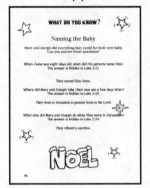

NOEL

46

Winter Wraps

overcoat   scarf   socks
boots   mittens   blanket
parka   sweater   ear muffs

47

WINTER WARM-UPS

ACROSS
4. A covering used on a bed
5. We wear them on our feet when we walk in the snow
6. These are knit coverings for our hands in cold weather
7. When we go out to play, we put on our _____
8. These go around our necks to keep us warm

DOWN
1. We wear these over our shirts for indoors or outdoors
2. Men wore these in the old days under their clothes
3. These are made of cloth or leather and keep our hands warm

50

GIVING THANKS

Fill in the missing letters to form a word or phrase from top to bottom.

F EAST
IND I ANS
CR A NBERRIES
S WEETPOTATOES
SWEE T CORN
T URKEY
PLYMOUTH
MA Y FLOWER
BEAN S
PUMPK I NPIE
S TUFFING
VE G ETABLES
FAM I LY
HAR V EST
SHARI N G
ACOR N
PIL G RIMS

51

Page 52

PICTURE THIS

Draw a line from each picture to its matching word in the middle. When you are through, a few words will be left over. Fill them into the line below to form a phrase.

Sleigh

present

bells

stocking

ornaments

toys

ring

Sleigh bells ring _____

52

Page 53

HOLIDAY SONGS

Find the missing word from the list below and finish the sentence

WE WISH YOU A MERRY CHRISTMAS

UP ON THE HOUSETOP

THERE'S A SONG IN THE AIR

THE HOLLY AND THE IVY

CHESTNUTS ROASTING ON AN OPEN FIRE

SONG   WISH   IVY

CHESTNUTS   HOUSETOP

53

Page 54

WHAT DO YOU KNOW?

Going to the Temple

Mary and Joseph made sure to dedicate Jesus to the Lord. Can you answer these questions?

Who did Mary and Joseph meet in the Temple in Jerusalem? The answer is hidden in Luke 2:25.

A man named Simeon.

What did Simeon do when he saw the Baby Jesus? The answer is hidden in Luke 2:28.

He took Jesus in his arms and blessed God for Him.

Simeon told Mary and Joseph that Jesus would be great and save us all. What did they do when they heard these words? The answer is hidden in Luke 2:33.

Mary and Joseph marveled at what Simeon said about Jesus

54

Page 55

Everyone Loves Snow

B	S	H	O	V	E	L	M
O	H	S	A	W	O	L	P
A	O	K	W	E	P	A	S
R	E	D	N	U	O	B	T
D	N	M	L	F	J	N	O
F	L	A	K	E	A	U	R
P	A	N	G	E	L	L	M
W	H	I	T	E	N	R	L

bell   flake   shovel
board   man   storm
bound   plow   angel
fall   shoe   white

55

Page 57

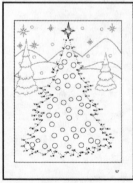

57

Page 58

THE HOLY BIRTH

ACROSS

7 This is where Mary placed the new-born king
8 This is the name of Jesus' mother
9 This is the name of Jesus' earthly father

DOWN

1. The wise men followed a _____
2. Mary rode to Bethlehem on a _____
3 There were no rooms so the baby was born in a _____
4. Mary and Joseph named the baby _____
5. There were _____ in the stable
6. The shepherds and wise men were looking for the _____

58

RING IN THE NEW

Fill in the missing letters to form a word or phrase from top to bottom.

HOR N S
CH E ERS
T W ELVE
JANUARY
GAM E S
PA R TIES
FI R EWORKS
FIR S T DAY
MI D NIGHT
H A TS
HAPP Y

HAPPY NEW YEAR

59

PICTURE THIS

Draw a line from each picture to its matching word in the middle. When you are through, a few words will be left over. Fill them into the line below to form a phrase.

holiday bells

Christmas tree

noel

first

The

snowflakes

teddy bear

The first noel

60

HOLIDAY SONGS

Find the missing word from the list below and finish the sentence.

O COME, O COME EMMANUEL

ALL I WANT FOR CHRISTMAS IS MY TWO FRONT TEETH

THE CHIPMUNK SONG

GRANDMA GOT RUN OVER BY A REINDEER

COME ON RING THOSE BELLS

REINDEER   FRONT TEETH   SONG
EMMANUEL   RING

Let it Snow

61

WHAT DO YOU KNOW?

Also in the Temple

After Simeon blessed Jesus and told His parents about Him, they met a woman named Anna. Can you answer these questions?

How old was the woman Joseph and Mary met in the Temple?
The answer is hidden in Luke 2:37.

Anna was 84 years old.

What did this woman do all day? The answer is hidden in Luke 2:37.

Anna served God by praying and fasting.

What did Anna do when she saw Jesus?
The answer is hidden in Luke 2:38.

Anna gave thanks to the Lord for Jesus.

62

Winter Words

B	F	R	O	S	T	Y	L
Y	L	L	I	H	C	T	X
S	L	U	S	H	M	P	I
P	A	N	S	D	L	O	C
Z	O	T	Y	T	O	L	Y
F	R	E	E	Z	E	A	F
D	N	Y	T	F	A	R	D
F	R	I	G	I	D	S	Y

blustery   drafty   frigid
chilly   freeze   frosty
cold snap   polar   icy
                       slush

63

65

CHRISTMAS CANDY

ACROSS
5. These tangy candies look like little white glitters
6. This is thick, sugary candy but non-square
7. These are chewy and come in shapes like fish and bears

DOWN
1. You break this candy into pieces. It usually has peanuts
2. These chewy candies come in different colors
3. This candy comes on a stick
4. These Christmas candies have stripes and hooks
5. This old fashioned candy sounds like it has fruit

66

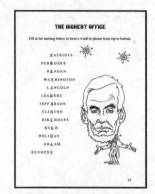

THE HIGHEST OFFICE

Fill in the missing letters to form a word or phrase from top to bottom.

PATRIOTS
FEBRUARY
REAGAN
WASHINGTON
LINCOLN
LEADERS
JEFFERSON
CLINTON
BIRTHDAYS
BUSH
HOLIDAY
OBAMA
KENNEDY

67

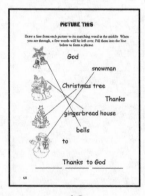

PICTURE THIS

Draw a line from each picture to its matching word in the middle. When you are through, a few words will be left over. Fill them into the line below to form a phrase.

God

snowman

Christmas tree

Thanks

gingerbread house

bells

to

Thanks to God

68

HOLIDAY SONGS

Find the missing word from the list below and finish the sentence.

IT'S THE MOST WONDERFUL TIME OF THE YEAR

WHAT CHILD IS THIS?

GO TELL IT ON THE MOUNTAIN

DECK THE HALLS

JOY TO THE WORLD

CHILD HALLS WORLD
MOUNTAIN WONDERFUL

Merry Christmas

69

WHAT DO YOU KNOW?

Who Is Jesus

Jesus, the Christ Child is the most important person in all the Bible. Long before He was born, God told people about Him. Can you answer these questions?

What name did God give to Jesus?
The answer is hidden in Isaiah 7:14.

Immanuel

What does the Bible say will be upon Jesus shoulders?
The answer is hidden in Isaiah 9:6.

The government

What tribe or clan does the Bible say Jesus will come from?
The answer is hidden in Micah 5:2.

Judah

70

Staying Warm

B	H	E	A	T		D	F		H
L		S	T	K	I	O	L		O
A	N	E	H	E	C	O	A		T
N	C	R	C	F	W	N	N		C
K	E	O	H	N	G	R	E		O
E	E	W	D	G	R		L		C
T	L	I	U	Q	I	L			O
M	F	E	R	I	F	N			A

blanket
quilt
flannel

fleece
firewood
heat

throw
coat
hot cocoa

71

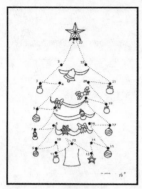

73

THE ANGEL'S SONG

ACROSS

5. The shepherds take care of the _____
6. The angels were called the _____ host
7. The angels sang _____ to God

DOWN

1. The sheep are cared for by the _____
2. The angels brought tidings of great _____
3. The _____ of the Lord shone round about the angels
4. The angels told the shepherds to _____
6. The angels were called the heavenly _____

74

READING WRITING ARITHMETIC

Fill in the missing letters, and the circled letters will form a word or phrase from top to bottom.

SCISSORS
PENCIL
TEACHER
BOOKS
NOTEBOOKS
GLUE
DESKS
ERASERS
CRAYONS
BUS

75

WHAT DO YOU KNOW?

The Christ Child

Can you answer these questions about the Christ Child?

Long before Jesus was born, God gave Him many titles. Can you name give of them hidden in Isaiah 9:6?

Wonderful
Counselor
Mighty God
Everlasting Father
Prince of Peace

When will God's Kingdom end? The answer is hidden in Isaiah 9:7.

His Kingdom will have no end.

78

Winter Holiday
New Year

glitter   confetti   hats
ball   January   midnight
kisses   parties   new
                             year

79

GIFT MAGIC

ACROSS

5. This sticky stuff keeps the paper in place
6. What we wrap the presents in
7. We write names on these and stick them to the presents
8. We use these to cut the paper to the right size

DOWN

1. We put the gifts in these before we wrap them
2. Before we can wrap the presents, we have to go _____
3. Another word for gifts
4. We use this kind of paper

82

83

SOUND SLEEPERS

Fill in the missing letters, and the circled letters will form a word or phrase from top to bottom.

This reindeer is Santa's favorite.

C H I P M U N K S
A N I M A L S
B E A R S
C A V E S
B E A R S
S N A I L S
B A T S
T U R T L E S
S L E E P I N G
W O O D C H U C K S
S N A K E S

83

84

PICTURE THIS

Draw a line from each picture to its matching word in the middle. When you are through, a few words will be left over. Fill them into the line below to form a phrase.

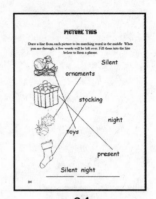

Silent

ornaments

stocking

night

toys

present

Silent night

84

86

WHAT DO YOU KNOW?

The Three Kings

Can you answer these questions about the three kings who came to visit the Christ Child?

These kings came to Jerusalem from faraway in the East. How did they find their way? The answer is hidden in Matthew 2:2.

They followed a star.

What did the three kings do when they found Jesus? The answer is hidden in Matthew 2:11.

They fell down and worshipped the Baby Jesus.

What gifts did the three kings bring to Jesus? The answer is hidden in Matthew 2:11.

Gold, frankincense, and myrrh.

86

87

Winter Holiday
Thanksgiving

W	I	S	H	B	O	N	E
L	N	L	Y	V	A	R	G
O	T	A	T	O	P	E	W
K	U	J	G	J	P	N	I
D	R	E	S	S	I	N	G
V	K	R	L	R	E	I	R
B	E	A	N	S	S	D	Y
W	Y	L	I	M	A	F	M

turkey   dressing   gravy
pies   wishbone   dinner
family   potato   beans

87

89

89

90

HOLIDAY CHEER

ACROSS
6. The First _____
8. The songs we sing at Christmas are called _____

DOWN
1. We like to ring these at Christmas
2. We sign and send these to our friends at Christmas
3. A time of prayer during the holidays
4. Mary laid Jesus in a _____ bed
5. We love to bake all kinds of these at Christmas
7. We wrap these around the tree and turn them on

90

WINTER WEATHER TERMS

Fill in the missing letters, and the circled letters will form a word or phrase from top to bottom.

H(A)IL
FLU(R)RIES
I(C)E
S(T)ORM
W(I)NDCHILL
(C)LOUDY
(F)ROST
C(O)LD
S(N)OWFALL
SLEE(T)

PICTURE THIS

Draw a line from each picture to its matching word in the middle. When you are through, a few words will be left over. Fill them into the line below to form a phrase.

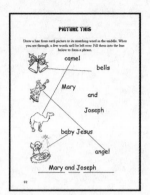

camel

bells

Mary

and

Joseph

baby Jesus

angel

Mary and Joseph

HOLIDAY SONGS

Find the missing word from the list below and finish the sentence.

IT'S BEGINNING TO LOOK A LOT LIKE CHRISTMAS

I HEARD THE BELLS ON CHRISTMAS DAY

LITTLE DRUMMER BOY

FELIZ NAVIDAD

O CHRISTMAS TREE

DRUMMER   FELIZ   CHRISTMAS

HEARD   LOOK

WHAT DO YOU KNOW?

Winter in the Bible

The Bible has a lot to say about wintertime.
Can you answer these questions?

What is as refreshing as a faithful messenger? The answer is hidden in Isaiah 55:13.

Faithful messengers are as refreshing as the cold of snow in the time of harvest.

What is it like when someone promises you a gift but doesn't give it to you? The answer is hidden in Isaiah 55:14.

Not giving a promised gift is like clouds and wind that don't bring rain.

What is it like when you sing a cheerful song to someone who is sad? The answer is hidden in Isaiah 55:20.

Singing cheerful songs to a sad person is like stealing someone's jacket in cold weather.

Winter Holiday Christmas

F	G	I	F	T	S	W	C	A
I	N	O	R	T	H	P	A	
R	E	I	N	D	E	E	R	
T	S	E	V	L	E	K	O	
R	S	L	E	I	G	H	L	
E	T	O	B	E	L	L	S	
E	A	P	A	T	N	A	S	
O	R	N	A	M	E	N	T	

santa   reindeer   ornament
gifts   sleigh   elves
north   fir trees   bells
pole   star   carols

HOLIDAY PIES

ACROSS

5. This is a nutty pie we like to make at Thanksgiving.
6. This pie is made with small, tart, red fruit
7. This pie sometimes has the word "meat" in it

DOWN

1. This pie is made from a stalk that grows in the North
2. This pie is made from a big, orange gourd
3. This pie is made from round, red fruit. It's the American pie
4. This pie has fluffy, white meringue on top

99

PILED HIGH

Fill in the missing letters, and the circled letters will form a word or phrase from top to bottom.

SAN(D)
FLURR(I)ES
STRENG(T)H
FRI(G)ID
DR(I)FTS
I(N)CHES
(G)LOVES
SH(O)VEL
SL(U)SH
BOO(T)S

102

Winter in the Bible

The Bible has a lot to say about wintertime. Can you answer these questions?

The Bible says that the "coming of refreshing rain in winter" is like what? The answer is hidden in Hosea 6:3.

Knowing the Lord.

The Bible says the "cold" comes from where? The answer is hidden in Job 37: 9.

The scattering winds of the north.

The Bible says "ice" comes from where? The answer is hidden in Job 37:10.

The breath of God.

103

Winter Sports

S	L	E	D	D	I	N	G	
K	H	L	O	R	S	E	N	
A	O	F	M	A	D	T	I	
T	C	R	G	O	E	A	K	
I	K	A	L	B	E	K	K	
N	E	J	U	M	P	S	S	
G	Y	N	G	Z	S	E	W	
S	H	O	E	S	B	L	X	

skating   jumps   hockey
sledding   board   skates
luge   skiing   speed
                                skate

105

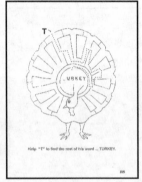

T

TURKEY

Help "T" to find the rest of his word ... TURKEY.

106

WINTER SIGHTS

SMOKEINTHECHIMNEY

ACROSS
7. We need to gather up _____ and twigs to start the fire
8. You can also crumple up _____ to start the fire

DOWN
1. That is blank and big enough to burn logs
2. This is made of brick and also burns logs
3. Fire warms up the air and gets rid of the _____
4. We stoke these to get the fire going
5. We can also use an electric _____ to warm up the room
6. We chop the wood into _____

107

MARY'S MIRACLE

Fill in the missing letters, and the circled letters will form a word or phrase from top to bottom.

This reindeer has a quick temper!

JE(S)US
NAT(I)VITY
ANGE(L)S
SHEPH(E)RDS
DON(N)KEY
S(T)AR
A(N)IMALS
KI(N)GOFKINGS
MA(N)GER
JOSEP(H)
BIR(T)H

PICTURE THIS

Draw a line from each picture to its matching word in the middle. When you are through, a few words will be left over. Fill them into the line below to form a phrase.

pie

stocking

A

manger

lamb

winter weather

bed

A manger bed

108

HOLIDAY SONGS

Find the missing word from the list below and finish the sentence.

HAVE YOURSELF A MERRY LITTLE CHRISTMAS

ANGELS WE HAVE HEARD ON HIGH

GOD REST YE MERRY GENTLEMEN

O COME ALL YE FAITHFUL

THE FIRST NOEL

FIRST   REST   FAITHFUL

MERRY   ANGELS

109

WHAT DO YOU KNOW?

Winter in the Bible

The Apostle Paul was arrested and sent to Rome on a ship where he would be put on trial. High winds and winter storms made the trip very dangerous. Can you answer these questions about Paul's winter journey?

Where did the ship finally stop?
The answer is hidden in Acts 27: 7-8.

A place called Fair Havens, near the city of Lasea.

When they left Fair Havens, Paul's ship set sail for what harbor in Crete? The answer is hidden in Acts 27: 12.

Phoenix, a harbor of Crete.

Everyone was afraid when the ship started to sink. What did Paul tell the frightened men who were on the ship with? The answer is hidden in Acts 27:22.

The ship would sink but all the people on board would be safe.

110

Winter Months

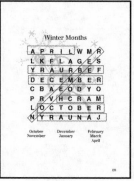

A	P	R	I	L	W	M	R
L	K	F	L	A	G	E	S
Y	R	A	U	R	B	E	F
D	E	C	E	M	B	E	R
C	B	A	E	O	D	Y	O
P	R	V	H	C	R	A	M
L	O	C	T	O	B	E	R
N	Y	R	A	U	N	A	J

October   December   February
November   January   March
                             April

111

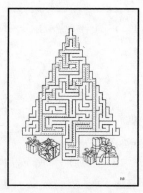

113

WINTER MONTHS

ACROSS
7. This is the month of Halloween
8. This month's showers wash the snow away

DOWN
1. This is the second month of the new year
2. This is the last month of winter
3. The winter months are not hot; they are _____
4. When we're cold we make this sound
5. This is the month of Thanksgiving
6. Winter is one of the four

114

JOSEPHS JOURNEY

Fill in the missing letters, and the circled letters will form a word or phrase from top to bottom.

This reindeer has a long tail.

M A G I
E G Y P T
H E R O D
N O R O O M
D O N K E Y
C H R I S T C H I L D
S H E P H E R D S
M A R Y
B I R T H
A N G E L S
S T A R
E M M A N U E L
N A T I V I T Y
J E S U S

115

PICTURE THIS

Draw a line from each picture to its matching word in the middle. When you are through, a few words will be left over. Fill them into the line below to form a phrase.

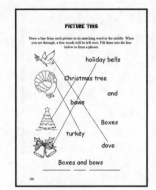

holiday bells

Christmas tree

and

bows

Boxes

turkey

dove

Boxes and bows

_____ _____ _____

116

HOLIDAY STORIES

Find the missing word from the list below and finish the sentence.

THE LITTLE MATCH GIRL

TWAS THE NIGHT BEFORE CHRISTMAS

CHRISTMAS AT THE CRATCHITS

THE ELVES AND THE SHOEMAKER

THE COBBLER'S NIGHT

ELVES   QUEST   CRATCHITS

LITTLE   NIGHT

117

WHAT DO YOU KNOW?

Winter in the Bible

The wind can be very cold in the winter time. Can you answer these questions about the wind?

When the winter winds and rain beat against the house built on the rock, did it fall or did it stand strong? The answer is hidden in Matthew 7:25.

It stood strong.

When the tall waves and winter wind started to sink the boat Jesus and His disciples were sailing in, Jesus stood up and spoke to the storm. What did Jesus say? The answer is hidden in Mark 4:37-38.

Jesus said, "Peace be still."

Where does the Bible say that God walks? The answer is hidden in Psalm 104:3.

God walks on the wings of the wind.

118

The Worst of Winter

B	L	U	S	T	E	R	Y
G	N	I	Z	E	E	R	F
I	C	E	S	T	O	R	M
T	H	C	H	I	L	L	W
E	O	U	C	O	L	D	I
E	B	L	E	A	K	C	N
L	K	F	R	I	G	I	D
S	N	I	F	F	L	E	S

blustery   freezing   ice storm
cold   bleak   sniffles
sleet   chill   flu
frigid

119

SIGNS OF SPRING

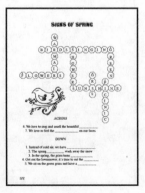

ACROSS

6. We love to stop and smell the beautiful _____
7. We love to feel the _____ on our faces

DOWN

1. Instead of cold air, we have _____
2. The spring _____ wash away the snow
3. In the spring, the grass turns _____
4. Get out the lawnmower, it's time to cut the _____
5. We sit on the green grass and have a _____

122

123

THE CHRISTMAS STORY

Fill in the missing letters, and the letters will form a word or phrase from top to bottom.

C H R I S T
H E A V E N L Y
K I N G
C R O S S
D I _ E
R E D E E M E R
P R O M I S E S
S A V I O R
S I _ _ E S
S O U L
J E S U S
L A M B O F G O D

124

PICTURE THIS

Draw a line from each picture to its matching word in the middle. When you are through, a few words will be left over. Fill them into the line below to form a phrase.

snowflake

holly   tree

the

Gifts

toys

under

wise men

Gifts under the __ ___

126

WHAT DO YOU KNOW?

Winter in the Bible

The Bible has a lot to say about wintertime. Can you answer these questions?

The Bible names five kinds of "weather." (Can you name them? The answer is hidden in Psalm 148:8.

Fire
Hail
Snow
Clouds
Stormy wind

What did all these types of weather do? The answer is hidden in Psalm 148:8.

God uses them to fulfill His Word.

127

Winter's End

W	A	R	M	A	I	R	K
U	R	A	E	F	S	U	N
S	T	I	L	L	E	S	U
M	N	T	O	T	E	N	N
O	O	K	I	W	K	E	E
O	U	D	N	E	G	R	R
L	B	E	G	R	H	T	T
B	I	R	D	S	O	N	G

green   warm air   buds
flowers   melting   sun
blooms   birdsong   rain
                            trees

129

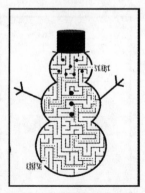

START

FINISH

130

STORMY WEATHER

W I N T E R W H I T E O U T

WINDY

BLIZZARD

RAIN

ACROSS
6. When the trees and the clouds are moving, it's _____
7. A really bad snowstorm is called a _____
8. Water from the clouds is called _____

DOWN
1. The snow piles up and makes _____
2. Winter winds blow in _____ air
3. In winter the roads can get _____
4. When rain freezes into hard chunks, we call it _____
5. Stormy weather can be very _____

WHO IS THAT MAN?

Fill in the missing letters, and the letters will form a word or phrase from top to bottom.

J U S T
H E A L E R
M E S S I A H
P U R E
C H R I S T
S A V I O R
L I V E
S I N L E S S
H O L Y
F R I E N D
K I N D
L O R D
R E D E E M E R

131

PICTURE THIS

Draw a line from each picture to its matching word in the middle. When you are through, a few words will be left over. Fill them onto the line below to form a phrase.

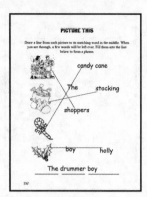

candy cane

The   stocking

shoppers

boy   holly

The drummer boy _____

132

WHAT DO YOU KNOW?

Winter in the Bible

The Bible uses snow to describe the whitest white of all. Can you answer these questions about things that are "as white as snow"?

What does the Bible say was "white as snow"? The answer is hidden in Daniel 7:9.

His garment.

What does the Bible say shall be as "white as snow"? The answer is hidden in Isaiah 1:18.

Our sins.

What does the Bible say God will do to make us "whiter than snow"? The answer is hidden in Psalm 51:7.

Wash me

134

Groundhog Day

F	O	R	E	C	A	S	T
E	L	W	A	T	C	H	C
B	K	S	L	P	N	A	I
R	E	T	N	I	W	D	D
U	D	A	Y	S	L	O	E
A	B	U	R	R	O	W	R
R	G	N	I	R	P	S	P
Y	W	E	A	T	H	E	R

burrow   spring   shadow
predict   weather   forecast
winter   watch   February

135

FAMILY FUN

T R I M M I N G T H E T R E E
C A N E
B E L L S
B O W S

ACROSS
6 Striped candy with a hook, these are candy _____
7 These are jingle _____ and silvery _____
8 These are made with brightly colored ribbon

DOWN
1 This goes on top of the tree
2 These are shiny strips of paper to brighten the tree
3 These come in all colors and flash off and on
4 These are under the tree to be opened on Christmas Day
5 These come in many shapes, colors, and stars

138

REINDEER TRACKS

Fill in the missing letters to form a word or phrase from top to bottom.

C U P I D
P R A N C E R
C O M E T
D A N C E R
B L I T Z E N
D A S H E R
V I X E N
R U D O L P H
D O N N E R
H O U S E
G I F T S
T R A C K S
S N O W
N O R T H P O L E

139

PICTURE THIS

Draw a line from each picture to its matching word in the middle. When you are through, a few words will be left over. Fill them into the line below to form a phrase.

drum

candle

the

Wrap

gifts

stocking

mittens

Wrap the gifts

140

140

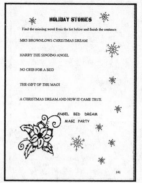

HOLIDAY STORIES

Find the missing word from the list below and finish the sentence.

MRS BROWNLOWS CHRISTMAS DREAM

HARRY THE SINGING ANGEL

NO CRIB FOR A BED

THE GIFT OF THE MAGI

A CHRISTMAS DREAM AND HOW IT CAME TRUE

ANGEL   BED   DREAM
MAGI   PARTY

141

141

WHAT DO YOU KNOW?

Winter in the Bible

The Bible has a lot to say about wintertime. Can you answer these questions?

The Bible says the "snow" is like what?
The answer is hidden in Psalm 147:16.

Wool.

In the same Psalm, the Bible says the "frost" is like what?
The answer is hidden in Psalm 147:16.

Ashes.

What is it God says to the "snow"? The answer is hidden in Job 37:9.

Fall on the earth.

142

142

Winter Birds

B	L	A	C	K	A	R	T
B	I	R	D	S	B	O	H
L	F	E	T	P	L	B	R
U	I	V	S	A	U	I	U
E	N	O	W	R	E	N	S
J	C	C	D	A	R	L	H
A	H	W	M	O	I	F	E
Y	S	R	W	W	T	O	S

black   wrens   robin
bird   finch   bluetit
bluejay   thrushes   sparrow
                       dove

143

143

145

145

PRESIDENTS DAY REVIEW

A M E R I C A N P R E S I D E N T S

F O R D

N I X O N

ACROSS
1 This president's name sounds like a car. His first name is Gerald
2 This president resigned from office. His first name is Richard

DOWN
1 This president was once a movie star. His first name was Ronald
2 This president's wife might also run for president. His first name is Bill
3 This president once lived on a peanut farm. His first name is Jimmy
4 This president was called Honest Abe. His first name is Abraham
5 This president was the first. His first name is George

146

146

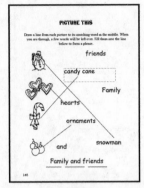

PICTURE THIS

Draw a line from each picture to its matching word in the middle. When you are through, a few words will be left over. Fill them into the line below to form a phrase.

friends

candy cane

Family

hearts

ornaments

snowman

and

Family and friends

148

HOLIDAY GREETINGS

Find the missing word from the list below and finish the sentence.

CHRISTMAS IS FOR CHILDREN

THE CHRISTMAS HEART IS A GIVING HEART

GOOD TIDINGS OF GREAT JOY

JESUS IS THE REASON FOR THE SEASON

THE JOY OF CHRISTMAS BRINGS US CLOSER TO EACH OTHER

GOD BLESS US EVERYONE!

BLESS   TIDINGS   CLOSER
HEART   CHILDREN   REASON

149

WHAT DO YOU KNOW?

Winter in the Bible

The Bible says that God is the only one who can control the weather. He decides when it will be cold and when it will be warm. Can you answer these questions?

What does the Bible say only God can do? The answer is hidden in Job 37:10.

Cover the sky with clouds so the sun can't shine through.

What does the Bible say only God can call down from heaven? The answer is hidden in Job 37:6.

He calls down the snow, the small rain and the great rain.

What is it the Bible says God's people are safe from even when this kind of weather comes down on them? The answer is hidden in Isaiah 32:18-19.

Hailstones

150

The Best of Winter

S	N	E	L	O	O	W	D
C	S	E	I	K	S	P	S
A	O	C	O	C	T	O	H
R	G	O	N	G	G	E	O
F	S	D	E	L	S	D	A
S	K	A	T	E	S	K	L
S	W	E	A	T	E	R	S
W	A	R	M	F	I	R	E

warm fire   scarfs   skiers
woolens   sweaters   sleds
hot cocoa   skates   eggnog

151

FINISH

153

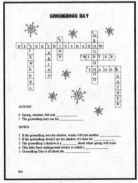

GROUNDHOG DAY

ACROSS

6 Spring, summer, fall and _____
7 The groundhog may see her _____

DOWN

1 If the groundhog sees his shadow, winter will last another _____
2 If the groundhog doesn't see his shadow, it's time for _____
3 The groundhog's shadow is a _____ about when spring will come
4 This little furry underground creator is called a _____
5 Groundhog Day is all about the _____

154

155

158

159

161

162

163

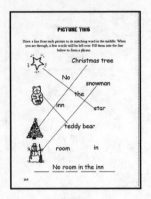

PICTURE THIS

Draw a line from each picture to its matching word in the middle. When you are through, a few words will be left over. Fill them into the line below to form a phrase.

Christmas tree

No

snowman

the

inn

star

teddy bear

room   in

No room in the inn _____

164

WHAT DO YOU KNOW?

Winter in the Bible

The Bible has a lot to say about wintertime.
Can you answer these questions?

Where do the "snow and rain" come from? The answer is hidden in Isaiah 55:10.

The snow and rain come down from the heavens.

How do the "rain and snow" make the Earth better? The answer is hidden in Isaiah 55:10.

They water the earth.
They make it bud and flourish.
They make it yield seed.

What does the Bible say is like the "rain and snow"? The answer is hidden in Isaiah 55:11

God's Word is like the rain and snow.

166

164   166